INNOVATIVE TEACHING AND LEARNING PEDAGOGY

Dr. Mrinmoy Mandal
Assistant Professor, Department of Chemistry,
School of Basic and Applied Sciences, Raffles University,
Neemrana-301705, Alwar, Rajasthan.

Dr. Naveen Kumar
Assistant Professor, Department of Zoology,
School of Basic and Applied Sciences, Raffles University,
Neemrana-301705, Alwar, Rajasthan.

Title : Innovative Teaching and Learning Pedagogy
Author : Dr. Mrinmoy Mandal, Dr. Naveen Kumar
Edition : First (July, 2024)
ISBN : 9788197792731

Published by

A Venture by -
PRACHI DIGITAL PUBLICATION

Regd. Add.: 254, Khuriyakhatta No. 10, Bindukhatta,
Lalkuan, Nainital - 262402, Uttarakhand, India
Website : www.taneeshapublishers.in
E-mail : taneeshapublishers@gmail.com
Phone : +91 845481 2712, +91 976041 7980

Printed by :
Manipal Technologies Limited, Bengaluru - 560001, Karnataka

ABOUT THE BOOK

"Innovative Teaching and Learning Pedagogy" is a comprehensive exploration of modern educational methodologies authored by Dr. Mrinmoy Mandal and Dr. Naveen Kumar, esteemed faculty members of Raffles University. This book emerges from a profound question about preparing students for the complexities of the contemporary world. It argues that traditional teaching methods, often centered on rote memorization and standardized testing, are inadequate for the dynamic needs of today's learners. Instead, the authors advocate for a holistic transformation in teaching approaches, integrating technology and fostering critical thinking and creativity.

The book is structured to guide educators through a variety of innovative pedagogical practices, emphasizing Student-centred learning environments that are interactive and engaging. Starting with a historical perspective, the book traces the evolution of education from ancient foundations through to the digital age, highlighting the significant shifts that have shaped current educational practices. The chapters delve into the pillars of innovative pedagogy, such as technology integration, project-based learning, flipped classrooms, experiential learning, and continuous assessment strategies. These methods are illustrated with practical examples and case studies that demonstrate their effectiveness in enhancing the learning experience.

The authors emphasize the role of teachers as architects of innovation, adapting to new roles as facilitators and mentors rather than mere knowledge transmitters. They highlight the importance of nurturing a growth mindset in educators, encouraging continuous professional development and collaboration within learning communities. Furthermore, the book addresses the challenges of resistance to change, offering strategies to overcome these barriers and create a culture of innovation within educational institutions. Special attention is given to inclusivity in the learning environment, advocating for differentiated instruction and personalized learning to cater to the diverse needs of all students. The integration of technology is presented not just as a tool but as a catalyst for educational transformation, with discussions on digital classrooms, e-learning platforms, virtual and augmented reality, and gamification. These technologies are shown to enhance accessibility, engagement, and the overall quality of education.

PREFACE

In the rapidly evolving landscape of education, the need for innovative teaching and learning pedagogy has never been more pressing. As we stand at the crossroads of technological advancements and educational demands, traditional methods of instruction are being challenged and reshaped. This book based on Innovative Teaching and Learning Pedagogy is a culmination of years of research, practice, and a deep-seated passion for transforming the educational experience.

The journey to writing this book began with a simple yet profound question: How can we better prepare our students for the complexities of the modern world? The answer, I discovered, lies not in a single strategy or approach but in a holistic transformation of our teaching methodologies. This book aims to explore and present a variety of innovative pedagogical practices that can enhance the learning experience, making it more engaging, effective, and relevant to the needs of today's learners.

Throughout the chapters, you will find a rich tapestry of ideas and strategies designed to inspire educators at all levels. From integrating technology in the classroom to fostering critical thinking and creativity, this book provides a comprehensive guide to reimagining education. The emphasis is on creating learning environments that are dynamic, interactive, and student-cantered, where learners are encouraged to take an active role in their educational journey.

CONTENTS

CHAPTER 1

INTRODUCTION

1.1 Background of Education Evolution

Evolution of Education: A Historical Overview

Education has always been a dynamic and transformative force, adapting to societal needs and demands. This chapter explores the evolution of education, reflecting cultural, economic, and technological changes throughout history.

I. Ancient Foundations:

Education's roots can be traced to ancient civilizations, where informal learning systems prevailed. In places like ancient Greece, Egypt, and China, education was often reserved for the elite and focused on philosophy, arts, and practical skills. These early systems set the stage for structured learning in later centuries.

II. Medieval Monasticism and Scholasticism:

In the Middle Ages, monasteries became centers of learning, preserving and transmitting knowledge through manuscript transcription. The rise of scholasticism in medieval universities marked a shift towards systematic education, blending theology with classical teachings.

III. Renaissance and Humanism:

The Renaissance revived interest in classical learning and human experience. Humanism emphasized education for personal development and civic engagement, promoting critical thinking, individualism, and a broader curriculum including humanities and sciences.

IV. The Age of Enlightenment:

The Enlightenment championed reason, science, and individual rights. Thinkers like John Locke and Jean-Jacques Rousseau saw education as key to cultivating rationality and moral character, influencing modern educational philosophy and the push for universal access to knowledge.

V. Industrial Revolution and Mass Education:

The 19th century Industrial Revolution necessitated a skilled workforce, leading to compulsory education systems. Public education made learning accessible to a broader population, marking a shift towards mass education.

VI. 20th Century Innovations:

The 20th century brought innovations like compulsory education, standardized testing, and progressive education movements. Technologies like radio, television, and computers introduced new teaching tools and mediums.

VII. Information Age and Digital Learning:

The 21st century's Information Age has revolutionized education through digital learning platforms, online courses, and interactive technologies. Education now emphasizes lifelong learning, adaptability, and technology integration to prepare individuals for a rapidly changing world.

1.2 The Urgency for Innovative Pedagogy

In today's rapidly evolving educational landscape, the call for innovative pedagogy has become a crucial response to the need for transforming traditional teaching methods. Long-standing educational practices are increasingly challenged by the dynamic demands of our fast-changing world. This urgency is driven by significant shifts in technology, societal expectations, and the global economy's demands.

The traditional education model, reliant on rote memorization, standardized tests, and lecture-based instruction, is now seen as inadequate for the 21st century. With vast information readily available, students must develop critical thinking, creativity, adaptability, and digital literacy to succeed in a technologically advanced and globally connected era.

Technology plays a pivotal role in this shift towards innovative pedagogy. The digital revolution has transformed how we access, share, and process information. Modern education now incorporates virtual classrooms, online collaboration platforms, interactive simulations, and immersive learning experiences, making technology an essential part of the learning process. This integration goes beyond mere modernization; it addresses the evolving needs of an information-driven society.

The changing nature of employment and societal needs further underscores the urgency for innovative pedagogy. The traditional focus on standardized testing and rote memorization often fails to prepare students for the modern workplace. Innovative teaching methods bridge the gap between theoretical knowledge and practical application, equipping students with the skills and mindset necessary for success in a dynamic global economy.

Recognizing diverse learning styles and the need for personalized education is also crucial. Each student brings unique strengths, challenges, and interests to the classroom. Traditional one-size-fits-all approaches are increasingly seen as insufficient. Innovative pedagogy embraces differentiated instruction, tailoring educational experiences to individual needs, thereby enhancing engagement and fostering inclusivity.

Innovative pedagogy represents a fundamental shift in educational philosophy, promoting a Student-centred approach that encourages curiosity, exploration, and active participation in knowledge construction. This contrasts with the traditional teacher-centric model, where information flows unidirectionally from teacher to student. Recognizing education as a dynamic, collaborative process between teachers and students underscores the urgency for innovative teaching methods.

Implementing these transformative changes in educational systems poses challenges, requiring concerted efforts from educators, institutions, and policymakers. Overcoming resistance to change, redefining assessment metrics, and investing in professional development are essential steps. However, the potential rewards are immense: a generation of learners prepared to face future complexities with resilience, creativity, and a passion for continuous learning.

1.3 Defining Key Terms: Innovation, Teaching, Learning, Pedagogy

In education, several key terms form the foundation of our understanding and practice. Here we defines and explores four pivotal terms: Innovation, Teaching, Learning, and Pedagogy. Understanding these terms is essential for navigating the evolving landscape of education, where new ideas, methods, and the dynamic interaction between educators and learners shape the learning experience.

I. **Innovation:** In education, innovation goes beyond introducing new technologies or methods. It involves the creative and purposeful generation of fresh ideas and their implementation to bring about positive change. Educational innovation encompasses inventive approaches, technologies, and methodologies that enhance the quality, relevance, and effectiveness of teaching and learning. Innovation fosters adaptability, creativity, and critical thinking.

II. **Teaching:** Teaching is the art and science of imparting knowledge, skills, and values from educators to learners. It involves guiding, facilitating, and inspiring the journey of acquiring understanding. Effective teaching extends beyond information transmission; it includes thoughtful planning, dynamic engagement, and creating a conducive learning environment. Teachers use diverse strategies, communication methods, and assessments tailored to meet students' unique needs.

III. **Learning:** Learning is a dynamic and transformative process through which individuals assimilate knowledge, skills, attitudes, and values. It involves the active construction of understanding, often through experiences, interactions, and reflection. Learning extends beyond traditional classrooms to include formal education, informal experiences, and self-directed exploration. It is a lifelong journey shaped by cultural contexts and individual experiences.

IV. **Pedagogy:** Pedagogy is the guiding philosophy and practice of teaching. It includes the methods, strategies, and principles educators use to facilitate effective learning. Pedagogy involves considerations for curriculum design, assessment strategies, classroom dynamics, and educational philosophy. Rooted in research and informed by an understanding of cognitive and social processes, pedagogy evolves with the expanding horizons of education, adapting to diverse contexts and subjects.

1.4 Influential Figures in Pedagogical Evolution

The evolution of pedagogy is a fascinating journey, shaped by the visionary contributions of influential figures who have significantly impacted the field of education. From ancient philosophers to modern innovators, these trailblazers have transformed teaching and learning and laid the groundwork for continuous educational advancements. This article explores the lives, philosophies, and contributions of ten key figures in pedagogical evolution.

- **Socrates (469-399 BCE):** Often considered the father of Western philosophy, Socrates introduced the Socratic method, engaging students in dialogue to promote critical thinking and self-discovery. His focus on inquiry and dialogue has profoundly influenced educational approaches for centuries.

- **Confucius (551-479 BCE):** In ancient China, Confucius emphasized moral character and ethical conduct in education. His teachings have shaped East Asian educational practices for millennia, focusing on virtues, social harmony, and holistic individual development.

- **Comenius (1592-1670):** John Amos Comenius, known as the "Father of Modern Education," championed universal education. His work, "The Great Didactic," promoted experiential learning, visual aids, and an integrated approach to subjects, laying the foundation for modern educational methods.
- **John Dewey (1859-1952):** A leader in the progressive education movement, John Dewey emphasized learning through experience and connecting education to real-life situations. His ideas on Student-centred learning and experiential education have significantly shaped modern educational practices.
- **Maria Montessori (1870-1952):** Maria Montessori revolutionized early childhood education with the Montessori Method, focusing on self-directed exploration, hands-on learning, and individualized instruction. Her approach has had a global influence, recognizing children's natural developmental stages.
- **Lev Vygotsky (1896-1934):** Lev Vygotsky's sociocultural theory emphasized the role of social interactions and cultural context in learning. His concept of the zone of proximal development has influenced modern practices such as scaffolding and collaborative learning.
- **Jean Piaget (1896-1980):** Jean Piaget's theory of cognitive development outlined stages of intellectual growth, providing a framework for understanding how individuals construct knowledge. His work has impacted curriculum design and the adaptation of teaching methods to students' cognitive stages.
- **Paulo Freire (1921-1997):** Paulo Freire, a Brazilian educator and philosopher, was a key figure in critical pedagogy. His work, "Pedagogy of the Oppressed," critiqued traditional education and advocated for a transformative, dialogical approach, empowering students through critical

thinking and dialogue.

- **Sugata Mitra (born 1952):** Sugata Mitra's "Hole in the Wall" experiments demonstrated children's ability to self-organize and learn through technology in unsupervised environments. His work has influenced discussions on self-directed learning and the role of technology in education.

The journey through the contributions of these influential figures reveals a rich tapestry of ideas that have shaped education. From ancient philosophies to modern technological advancements, these visionaries have left an enduring mark on how we perceive teaching and learning. Their legacies inspire educators and policymakers to build upon these foundations and propel pedagogy toward a future of innovation, inclusivity, and transformative learning experiences.

CHAPTER 2

THE PILLARS OF INNOVATIVE PEDAGOGY

2.1 Student-centred Learning

In modern education, Student-centred Learning stands as a transformative approach, shifting the focus from teachers to learners. This method redefines teaching and learning by placing students at the heart of their educational experience. Student-centred Learning emphasizes autonomy, giving students the power to shape their academic paths and take ownership of their learning outcomes. Collaboration is key, encouraging students to share ideas and solve problems together, creating an interactive learning community. Personalization addresses individual learning styles and preferences, while inquiry-based learning fosters critical thinking through exploration and discovery.

The benefits of Student-centred Learning are widespread, affecting both students and teachers. Students, empowered to make choices and set goals, show greater engagement and a positive attitude towards education. They develop critical thinking skills and retain knowledge more effectively, fostering a lifelong commitment to learning. Teachers become facilitators, guiding students through their educational journey and tailoring instruction to meet diverse needs. This approach enhances classroom dynamics, promoting collaboration, interaction, and mutual respect, and allows educators to address individual student needs more effectively.

Implementing Student-centred Learning requires a shift in mindset and instructional strategies. Educators must adopt flexible and adaptable methods, moving away from traditional authoritarian roles. Inquiry-based and project-based learning become central, encouraging students to explore and apply knowledge in real-world scenarios. Technology plays a crucial role, offering tools and resources for personalized learning experiences. Learning Management Systems help organize content, track progress, and facilitate communication between students and teachers, making the implementation of Student-centred Learning more efficient and effective.

2.2 Active Learning model

Active learning models represent a dynamic shift in education, moving away from passive reception towards a more engaging, participatory approach. This exploration delves into the multifaceted nature of active learning, examining its principles, diverse models, and the transformative impact on both students and educators.

At its core, active learning challenges traditional education, emphasizing that students learn best when they actively participate. This shift from the conventional lecture-based format redefines the roles of both educators and learners, fostering an interactive environment that promotes critical thinking, problem-solving, and deeper understanding.

The principles of active learning are rooted in constructivist theories, asserting that knowledge is actively built by the learner. This approach recognizes the diverse backgrounds, learning styles, and prior knowledge students bring. By incorporating active learning strategies, educators create an inclusive and adaptive learning ecosystem.

Active learning takes various forms, each with unique characteristics. One prominent model is problem-based learning (PBL), where students tackle real-world issues, collaborate to identify problems, conduct research, and propose solutions. PBL cultivates subject-specific knowledge and hones critical thinking, teamwork, and communication skills.

Another influential model is flipped learning, where traditional lecture and homework elements are reversed. Students engage with instructional content independently outside of class, freeing up class time for interactive activities and discussions. This model enhances student-teacher interactions and provides a personalized learning experience.

Collaborative learning emphasizes group activities where students work together to achieve common goals. This model fosters social skills and encourages diverse perspectives, leading to a richer understanding of the subject matter. Peer instruction, a form of collaborative learning, involves students teaching each other, reinforcing their own understanding and promoting shared responsibility.

Incorporating active learning models requires a deliberate and strategic approach. Educators must value student engagement and the co-construction of knowledge, shifting their role to guides and facilitators. Implementation strategies include interactive activities, such as case studies, simulations, debates, and hands-on experiments. Utilizing technology, educators can integrate online platforms and multimedia resources to enhance active learning experiences. Assessment methods should measure not just memorization but also the application, analysis, and synthesis of knowledge.

2.3 The Integration of Technology

Integrating technology into teaching and learning marks a significant shift in education, offering a transformative vision for the future. In today's dynamic educational landscape, technology plays a crucial role in enhancing pedagogical approaches, creating a more engaging, inclusive, and effective learning environment.

Technology is not just a supplement but a fundamental part of reshaping the educational experience. Tools like interactive smart boards, virtual reality simulations, and online collaboration platforms are revolutionizing how educators deliver lessons. These technologies enable the creation of immersive and interactive lessons that cater to diverse learning styles, making education more personalized and dynamic.

One major advantage of technology integration is the facilitation of personalized learning experiences. Adaptive learning platforms use algorithms and data analytics to tailor instruction to individual student needs. By tracking progress and adjusting content, these platforms provide customized learning paths, accommodating different learning paces and fostering a sense of autonomy and engagement among students.

Technology also extends learning opportunities beyond traditional classrooms and geographical boundaries. Online platforms and collaborative tools connect students with peers worldwide, promoting global perspectives and cross-cultural collaboration. Virtual exchange programs and international projects become integral parts of education, preparing students for a digitally connected world.

Moreover, technology enhances the accessibility of educational resources. Digital textbooks, online libraries, and open educational resources make quality learning materials available to a broader audience, helping bridge educational disparities. Students from diverse socio-economic backgrounds can benefit from these resources, democratizing access to knowledge.

In assessment and feedback, technology offers innovative solutions beyond traditional exams. Online quizzes, interactive assessments, and gamified learning platforms provide real-time feedback, enabling timely interventions. E-portfolios and multimedia projects allow students to showcase their skills creatively, moving beyond traditional paper-and-pencil assessments.

However, integrating technology comes with challenges. Ensuring equitable access to technology, addressing data privacy concerns, and fostering digital literacy skills are essential. Educators must navigate these challenges thoughtfully to ensure that all students benefit from technology integration, regardless of their socio-economic background or location.

2.4 Inclusivity in the Learning Environment

Inclusivity in the learning environment is a core principle that ensures effective and equitable education. It requires active efforts to create a space where everyone, regardless of background or abilities, feels valued and can fully participate in learning. Inclusive education covers a wide range of aspects, including race, ethnicity, gender, socioeconomic status, language proficiency, and abilities. The benefits are extensive, enriching the educational experience and developing socially responsible and empathetic citizens.

A key aspect of an inclusive learning environment is recognizing and celebrating diversity. Educators must acknowledge the unique backgrounds and perspectives of students, creating a curriculum that reflects this diversity. This approach helps students see themselves in the content, fostering a sense of belonging. Exposure to diverse perspectives also broadens students' understanding of the world and prepares them for global challenges.

Differentiated instruction is essential for inclusivity. Recognizing that students have different learning styles and needs, educators should tailor their approaches to accommodate these differences. This might involve using various methods of representation, engagement, and expression. Technology can support this by offering adaptive learning platforms and assistive tools. By embracing differentiation, educators ensure that all students can thrive.

Creating an inclusive learning environment also means addressing systemic barriers that limit participation. This requires a commitment to equity, where educators examine and rectify biases in their practices and policies. Inclusivity aligns with social justice, aiming to provide equal opportunities for all students through anti-bias education and culturally responsive teaching.

Inclusivity extends to social and emotional well-being. Building positive relationships among students and between students and educators is crucial. Social-emotional learning (SEL) programs can foster empathy, communication, and conflict resolution skills, helping students contribute to an inclusive community.

Supporting students with diverse abilities is another aspect of inclusivity. This involves providing accommodations and accessible resources to ensure full participation. Universal Design for Learning (UDL) principles guide educators in creating flexible environments that meet diverse needs. Promoting empathy and understanding helps reduce stigmas associated with disabilities.

Collaboration with families and the community is vital for sustaining inclusivity. Educators should involve parents and community members in the educational process, seeking their input and incorporating their perspectives. Strong partnerships with families and communities create a supportive network that enhances the learning environment's inclusivity.

2.5 Continuous Assessment Strategies

Continuous assessment strategies are emerging as dynamic and effective methods for evaluating student learning over time, moving beyond traditional summative assessments. This shift involves the ongoing collection and analysis of student performance, giving educators a comprehensive view of individual progress and enabling timely interventions. Unlike conventional exams, which often measure knowledge retention at a single point, continuous assessments recognize the evolving nature of learning and aim to capture a more nuanced understanding of a student's abilities.

The core idea of continuous assessment is that learning is an ongoing and dynamic process, and evaluation methods should reflect this. Formative assessment, a key part of this approach, occurs throughout the learning process, offering feedback to both educators and students. This real-time feedback loop allows for immediate adjustments, helping educators tailor their instruction and aiding learners in tracking their progress and identifying areas for improvement.

One notable continuous assessment strategy is the use of formative quizzes and low-stakes assessments. These assessments, conducted regularly, serve to gauge understanding and reinforce learning objectives. By providing immediate feedback, educators can address misconceptions promptly and adapt their teaching strategies to ensure mastery of key concepts. The low-stakes nature of these assessments reduces stress and fosters a growth mindset, encouraging students to see mistakes as opportunities for learning.

Another key component of continuous assessment is project-based assessments. These require students to apply their knowledge and skills in real-world scenarios, moving beyond rote memorization. Projects can include research papers, presentations, or hands-on experiments, allowing students to showcase their understanding and creativity. These projects are assessed holistically, evaluating critical thinking, problem-solving, collaboration, and communication skills.

Peer assessment is also gaining prominence as a valuable tool in continuous assessment strategies. This involves students evaluating their peers' work, fostering a sense of shared responsibility for learning. Through peer assessment, students receive diverse perspectives on their work and develop skills in constructive criticism and self-reflection. This collaborative approach enhances the learning experience by promoting engagement and active participation.

The incorporation of technology into continuous assessment strategies is increasingly prevalent, offering innovative ways to collect, analyze, and share assessment data. Learning management systems provide platforms for online quizzes, discussion forums, and collaborative projects, enabling educators to track student progress and engagement. Adaptive learning technologies personalize learning pathways based on individual performance, tailoring the educational experience to meet each student's needs. Data analytics tools allow educators to identify trends in student performance, informing instructional decisions and interventions.

Peer feedback and self-assessment are crucial components of continuous assessment, empowering students to take an active role in their learning journey. Peer feedback involves students providing constructive comments on their classmates' work, fostering a sense of community and collective growth. Self-assessment encourages students to reflect on their strengths and areas for improvement, promoting metacognition and self-regulation. These reflective processes help students develop a deeper understanding of their learning and take ownership of their academic progress.

A dynamic aspect of continuous assessment is the use of reflective journals and portfolios. Students document their learning experiences, challenges, and achievements, creating a narrative that showcases their academic and personal growth. These portfolios serve as a holistic assessment tool, allowing educators to assess cognitive skills as well as the development of critical thinking, communication, and self-directed learning.

Aligning continuous assessment with learning outcomes and curriculum standards is essential. Educators must clearly define the desired outcomes and competencies, ensuring that assessment strategies effectively measure these benchmarks. This alignment promotes transparency and fairness, reinforcing the purpose of assessment as a tool for gauging the attainment of educational goals.

CHAPTER 3

TEACHERS AS ARCHITECTS OF INNOVATION

3.1 The Changing Role of Teachers

The evolving role of teachers in innovative teaching and learning reflects a significant shift from traditional models where educators were primarily knowledge providers. Today, teachers are seen as facilitators of dynamic, Student-centred learning experiences. No longer confined to delivering information, teachers now act as catalysts for inquiry, guides in the learning process, and mentors who inspire critical thinking and creativity. With technology reshaping education, teachers are expected to master not only subject matter but also the use of technology to enhance learning outcomes.

A key aspect of this new role is facilitating Student-centred learning. Instead of relying on traditional lectures, teachers now create environments that empower students to take an active role in their learning. This approach acknowledges that each student is unique, with distinct strengths and learning paces. Teachers are using strategies that promote autonomy, collaboration, and personalized learning paths, fostering a deeper understanding and a lifelong love for learning.

In innovative pedagogy, teachers are seen as learning experience designers. They create engaging and immersive lessons using technology, experiential learning, and real-world applications. Design thinking, project-based learning, and inquiry-based methods are essential tools, enabling teachers to cater to diverse interests and learning styles. This requires educators to integrate interdisciplinary concepts and real-world connections into their teaching practices.

Technology integration is a defining feature of the modern teaching role. Teachers navigate a digital landscape filled with interactive tools, multimedia resources, and online platforms. Their role as technology integrators involves staying updated with advancements and leveraging these tools to create dynamic and customized learning environments. Virtual simulations, collaborative online projects, and adaptive learning platforms are examples of how technology is used to meet students' diverse needs.

Collaboration and communication skills are crucial in Student-centred learning environments. Teachers guide students in meaningful interactions and teamwork, while also connecting with professional learning networks to share best practices globally. Effective communication with students, parents, and colleagues is a hallmark of the modern educator, essential for navigating an interconnected world.

The role of teachers also focuses on fostering 21st-century skills like critical thinking, creativity, communication, and collaboration. These skills are vital for success in a rapidly changing global landscape. Teachers integrate project-based learning, problem-solving activities, and real-world scenarios to help students develop these crucial skills.

Assessment and feedback have also evolved. Teachers are moving beyond traditional tests to incorporate formative assessments that provide ongoing feedback. This approach measures not only knowledge but also skills, competencies, and real-world application. A holistic approach to assessment includes project outcomes, collaborative contributions, and reflective portfolios, offering a comprehensive view of student achievement.

Continuous professional development is essential for teachers. Staying current with pedagogical trends, technological advancements, and innovative strategies is a professional imperative. Workshops, conferences, and online courses help teachers refine their skills, exchange ideas, and stay informed about the latest educational research, modeling the value of lifelong learning for their students.

3.2 Nurturing a Growth Mindset in Educators

Fostering a growth mindset among educators is crucial for shaping professional development and learning environments in educational institutions. Coined by psychologist Carol S. Dweck, the concept emphasizes the belief that abilities and intelligence can be developed through dedication and perseverance. In education, cultivating a growth mindset encourages continuous learning and resilience, shifting away from fixed notions of ability towards embracing challenges as opportunities for personal and professional growth.

This shift encourages educators to view learning as a lifelong journey, motivating them to seek new knowledge, refine teaching strategies, and adapt to evolving educational landscapes. This mindset not only influences instructional practices and classroom dynamics but also fosters a supportive school culture where collaboration and continuous improvement are valued. Educators with a growth mindset are more likely to experiment with innovative teaching methods, incorporate technology, and adapt their approaches to meet diverse student needs. They create classrooms that nurture curiosity and encourage students to view mistakes as part of the learning process, fostering both academic and socio-emotional development.

Furthermore, fostering a growth mindset involves creating communities where educators can collaborate, share experiences, and support each other's professional growth. Mentorship programs and institutional support are instrumental in providing guidance and resources that empower educators to embrace challenges and strive for continuous improvement. By prioritizing professional development and recognizing achievements, educational institutions cultivate an environment where educators feel valued and motivated to contribute to the collective growth of their learning community.

3.3 Professional Development for Innovative Teaching

Professional development aimed at fostering innovative teaching practices stands as a cornerstone in the evolution of education, propelling educators into a realm where creativity, adaptability, and technology converge to shape dynamic learning experiences. In today's rapidly changing educational landscape, the need for teachers to stay updated on innovative pedagogies, emerging technologies, and evolving educational theories is more critical than ever. Innovative teaching transcends traditional methods, embracing a Student-centred approach that harnesses technology, encourages critical thinking, and prepares learners for the complexities of the 21st century.

At its heart, professional development for innovative teaching seeks to instill a growth mindset among educators. This mindset, rooted in the belief that abilities and intelligence can be developed through dedication and hard work, is essential for embracing classroom innovation. Through targeted workshops, seminars, and collaborative learning experiences, educators are introduced to the principles of a growth mindset and encouraged to view challenges as opportunities for learning and improvement. This foundational shift in mindset forms the basis for all aspects of innovative teaching, fostering a culture of continuous improvement and flexibility.

In the realm of innovative teaching, technology serves as a driving force, and professional development plays a crucial role in ensuring educators are proficient in its integration. Workshops focusing on technology-enhanced learning, virtual classrooms, and digital tools equip educators with the skills to create engaging and interactive learning environments. Whether exploring virtual reality simulations, gamified learning platforms, or collaborative online spaces, teachers gain insights into how technology can effectively engage students and enrich their learning experiences. Furthermore, professional development offers educators a platform to exchange best practices, address challenges, and collaboratively discover innovative methods to leverage technology to accommodate diverse learning styles and preferences.

Innovative teaching thrives on pedagogical approaches that depart from traditional norms. Professional development initiatives delve into methodologies such as project-based learning, inquiry-based learning, and flipped classrooms. Workshops guide educators through designing and implementing project-based units, where students engage in real-world problem-solving, critical thinking, and teamwork. Similarly, inquiry-based learning workshops empower teachers to facilitate student-driven exploration and investigation, fostering a genuine passion for learning beyond rote memorization. The flipped classroom model, which reverses traditional homework and lecture elements, becomes a focal point of professional development, encouraging educators to create interactive and collaborative in-class activities that maximize face-to-face learning opportunities.

Collaborative learning experiences are integral to professional development for innovative teaching, reflecting a shift towards Student-centred education. Educators participate in collaborative projects, peer observations, and interdisciplinary collaborations to break down barriers and cultivate a culture of shared learning. This collaborative spirit extends beyond workshops, creating a community where educators continually exchange ideas, resources, and strategies. The strength of collaborative learning lies not only in skill acquisition but also in creating a supportive environment where educators feel empowered to take risks, share insights, and collectively advance teaching practices.

Another crucial aspect of professional development for innovative teaching is the focus on socio-emotional learning (SEL) and culturally responsive teaching. Training sessions and workshops explore strategies for fostering inclusive and emotionally supportive classrooms. Educators learn to integrate SEL into their teaching, nurturing students' social and emotional well-being alongside academic growth. Additionally, professional development emphasizes culturally responsive teaching, guiding educators to develop instructional materials that respect and reflect the diverse backgrounds of their students. This deliberate emphasis on SEL and cultural responsiveness ensures that innovative teaching approaches are not only effective but also equitable and inclusive.

Assessment strategies are also transformed within professional development for innovative teaching. Traditional summative assessments give way to formative assessments that offer real-time feedback to students, guiding their learning journey. Educators explore alternative assessment methods like project portfolios, peer evaluations, and self-assessments, aligning with the principles of innovative teaching to capture a comprehensive understanding of student progress. Workshops guide teachers in designing assessments that assess not just knowledge but also critical thinking, creativity, and problem-solving skills.

Continuous reflection and self-assessment are crucial elements of professional development for innovative teaching. Educators engage in reflective practices that prompt them to evaluate their teaching methods critically, experiment with new approaches, and refine instructional strategies. Professional development programs provide spaces for teachers to share their reflections, seek feedback, and continually improve their practice. Emphasizing a growth mindset, central to innovative teaching, educators perceive challenges and setbacks as opportunities for learning and growth.

Administrative support and leadership are pivotal in shaping professional development for innovative teaching. Educational leaders must prioritize and invest in ongoing professional development, recognizing its transformative impact on teaching quality and student outcomes. Leadership initiatives that encourage innovation, celebrate risk-taking, and provide resources for continuous learning bolster the success of professional development efforts. Moreover, leadership support is essential in crafting a unified vision for innovative teaching across the school, ensuring alignment with institutional goals and promoting a cohesive approach to educational advancement.

3.4 Cultivating Collaborative Learning Communities

Creating collaborative learning communities within educational settings is a transformative effort that redefines traditional approaches to teaching and learning. These communities are built on the idea of educators, students, and sometimes parents actively engaging in shared learning experiences, exchanging ideas, and working together to enhance educational outcomes. This collaborative approach fosters a sense of collective responsibility for the success and well-being of all participants, recognizing that learning is a social and dynamic process that thrives on diverse perspectives and collaborative problem-solving.

Central to cultivating collaborative learning communities is the establishment of professional learning communities (PLCs) among educators. These collaborative spaces provide opportunities for educators to share best practices, discuss teaching strategies, and address challenges collectively. PLCs support ongoing professional development through reflective dialogue and exploration of innovative teaching methods, enriching both individual growth and overall teaching quality within schools or districts.

Additionally, fostering collaborative learning communities involves promoting shared leadership and decision-making. Educators assume leadership roles based on their expertise and interests, empowering them to contribute effectively to community goals. Decision-making processes include input from various stakeholders, ensuring decisions are informed by diverse perspectives and fostering a sense of ownership among all community members.

Student involvement is integral to collaborative learning communities, encouraging collaboration through group projects, peer learning, and problem-solving activities. This approach not only enhances academic collaboration but also develops students' socio-emotional skills, preparing them for success in a connected world. Similarly, involving parents as partners in education beyond traditional roles strengthens collaborative efforts and supports a holistic learning environment.

In the digital age, technology plays a vital role in facilitating collaboration within learning communities. Online platforms and tools enable communication and engagement among members, overcoming geographical barriers and promoting asynchronous collaboration. Virtual learning communities provide spaces for educators to share resources and discuss innovative practices, while students benefit from online tools that facilitate remote teamwork and idea exchange.

Physical spaces also contribute to cultivating collaborative learning environments. Flexible learning environments with adaptable furniture and technology integration encourage dynamic group activities and project-based learning. These spaces promote spontaneous interactions and cross-disciplinary collaboration, fostering creativity and a sense of community among learners.

Assessment within collaborative learning communities adopts a comprehensive approach, incorporating formative assessments, peer evaluations, and self-assessments. Educators use diverse assessment methods to measure content knowledge, critical thinking, communication, and collaboration skills. Feedback is integral to the learning process, supporting continuous improvement and valuing the journey of learning alongside academic achievements.

Building trust, promoting open communication, and embracing diversity are essential to cultivating collaborative learning communities. Establishing norms for respectful collaboration and culturally responsive practices ensures inclusivity and values the unique contributions of all community members. Administrative support is crucial, providing leadership, resources, and structures that foster a collaborative culture and recognize the contributions of educators, students, and parents alike.

3.5 Overcoming Resistance to Change

Overcoming resistance to change in innovative teaching and learning pedagogy is a complex but essential endeavor as educators navigate a landscape shaped by new technologies, evolving educational theories, and a shift towards Student-centred learning. Traditional educational practices sometimes face resistance from educators who are comfortable with established methods and skeptical about the benefits of new approaches. Addressing and understanding the sources of this resistance are critical steps towards fostering a culture that embraces transformative teaching practices.

One common source of resistance is fear of the unknown. Educators may worry about how innovative teaching methods will affect their roles, teaching styles, and classroom dynamics. Clear communication that explains the reasons for change, the potential advantages for educators and students alike, and the available support systems is crucial. Providing professional development opportunities that equip educators with the skills and knowledge needed for innovative pedagogy helps them approach new methodologies with confidence.

Another key aspect of overcoming resistance is addressing concerns related to perceived loss of control. Educators may resist change if they feel that innovative pedagogy undermines their autonomy or challenges their authority in the classroom. Empowering educators through collaborative decision-making, involving them in designing and implementing new practices, and emphasizing their expertise in shaping the learning environment can alleviate concerns and foster a sense of ownership in the change process.

Resistance may also stem from a lack of understanding or insufficient training in new teaching methodologies such as project-based learning or flipped classrooms. Effective professional development programs provide comprehensive training, ongoing support, and opportunities for collaborative learning. By addressing practical implementation challenges, offering resources, and creating a supportive community where educators can share insights and challenges, institutions can help educators overcome resistance and successfully integrate innovative teaching strategies.

Institutional culture plays a significant role in either promoting or inhibiting resistance to change. Educational institutions that prioritize continuous improvement, experimentation, and openness to new ideas are more likely to embrace innovative teaching practices. Leaders should assess and, if necessary, transform institutional culture to one that values creativity, adaptability, and a growth mindset. Recognizing and celebrating successes within the institution reinforces the value of innovation and contributes to a culture that views change positively.

Aligning innovative teaching practices with the broader mission and values of the educational institution is essential for overcoming resistance.

Educators are more likely to embrace change if they see how innovative pedagogy enhances the institution's mission, supports educational goals, and aligns with its core values. Establishing a clear connection between innovative teaching methods and institutional objectives helps educators understand the broader purpose and significance of the change.

Another dimension of resistance arises when educators perceive a lack of support, resources, or recognition for their efforts in adopting innovative teaching methods. Leaders must address these concerns by allocating resources for professional development, providing technological infrastructure, and acknowledging the efforts of educators who embrace innovative pedagogy. Support mechanisms such as mentorship programs and opportunities for collaboration create a positive environment where educators feel valued and motivated to explore and implement new teaching practices.

Moving towards Student-centred learning from a more traditional teacher-centered approach can also provoke resistance among educators unfamiliar with or uncomfortable with this shift. Professional development programs should focus on explaining the principles of Student-centred learning, offering theoretical frameworks, practical strategies, and examples of successful implementation. Highlighting the benefits of a Student-centred approach, such as increased engagement, deeper understanding, and improved critical thinking skills, can help educators see the positive outcomes for both them and their students.

Leadership plays a crucial role in overcoming resistance to change in innovative teaching and learning pedagogy. Educational leaders must advocate for and model innovative practices, inspiring and motivating educators to embrace change. Demonstrating a commitment to ongoing learning and showcasing successful implementations of innovative pedagogy contribute to a culture where innovation is valued and supported. Additionally, leaders should listen actively to educators' concerns and feedback, fostering a collaborative approach that includes their voices in decision-making processes.

Effective communication strategies are essential for overcoming resistance in innovative teaching and learning pedagogy. Leaders should use various communication channels to keep educators well-informed about the goals, benefits, and progress of change initiatives. Open and transparent communication builds trust, reduces uncertainty, and addresses the fear of the unknown associated with change. Creating opportunities for dialogue, such as town hall meetings, discussion groups, and digital platforms, allows educators to express concerns, share experiences, and contribute to ongoing conversations about innovative pedagogy.

CHAPTER 4

TECHNOLOGY AS AN EDUCATIONAL CATALYST

4.1 Digital Classrooms: Beyond the Basics

Digital classrooms have evolved into more than mere content delivery platforms; they now embody a revolutionary approach to innovative teaching and learning. Beyond integrating technology into the curriculum, modern digital classrooms are dynamic spaces where educators harness technology's power to boost student engagement, collaboration, and personalized learning experiences. A pivotal aspect of advancing digital classrooms involves embracing interactive and immersive technologies. Tools like virtual and augmented reality allow students to explore subjects in three-dimensional settings, enhancing their understanding and retention. By immersing students in real-world scenarios, these technologies transform them from passive learners into active participants in their educational journey, offering engagement levels and experiential learning opportunities previously unimaginable.

Additionally, the integration of artificial intelligence (AI) and machine learning algorithms propels digital classrooms to new heights. These intelligent systems analyses extensive student data to identify individual learning patterns, preferences, and areas needing improvement. Educators use this data to tailor instruction, offer targeted interventions, and create personalized learning paths. AI-powered adaptive learning platforms enable students to progress at their own pace, ensuring each learner receives the necessary support and challenges. In this way, digital classrooms become not just repositories of information but responsive ecosystems that adapt to each student's unique needs, fostering a more inclusive and effective learning environment.

Collaborative features within digital classrooms facilitate communication and teamwork among students, transcending geographical barriers. Online discussion forums, collaborative document editing, and virtual project spaces enable meaningful interactions regardless of students' locations. Educators utilize these tools to foster a sense of community and shared learning experiences. Moreover, synchronous and asynchronous communication channels accommodate diverse learning styles. Through video conferencing, live chats, and discussion boards, students engage in class discussions, seek clarification, and collaborate on assignments, enhancing connectivity and shared intellectual exploration.

Gamification represents another innovative facet of digital classrooms that goes beyond basic technology integration. Elements such as badges, rewards, and interactive simulations transform learning into an engaging and motivating experience. Educators employ game-based learning to introduce competition, exploration, and problem-solving into the curriculum. Gamification captures students' attention and promotes intrinsic motivation, critical thinking, and perseverance-skills crucial in today's complex world. By leveraging game design principles, digital classrooms become dynamic environments where learning is active, enjoyable, and participatory rather than passive absorption of information.

Advanced digital classrooms also revolutionize assessment tools, departing from traditional evaluation methods. These tools enable educators to assess not only content knowledge but also higher-order thinking skills, creativity, and problem-solving abilities. Formative assessment platforms provide real-time feedback, allowing educators to address misconceptions promptly and adjust teaching strategies. Furthermore, digital assessment tools facilitate authentic assessments like multimedia projects and online portfolios, which align better with the skills demanded in the digital age. For instance, e-portfolios enable students to showcase their talents, achievements, and reflections on their learning journey, fostering a comprehensive approach to assessment.

Cybersecurity and digital literacy are integral in advanced digital classrooms. Beyond using digital tools, students must understand online safety, responsible digital citizenship, and ethical information use. Educators guide students through these complexities, teaching them to critically evaluate online information, navigate digital platforms responsibly, and protect their privacy. In advanced digital classrooms, the curriculum extends beyond subject-specific content to encompass explicit instruction on digital literacy, equipping students with essential skills for thriving in an interconnected, information-rich world.

Moreover, advanced digital classrooms embrace the flipped classroom model, redefining traditional in-class and out-of-class activities. By creating online instructional materials such as video lectures, podcasts, and interactive simulations, educators move content delivery outside the classroom. This approach allows valuable in-class time for collaborative activities, discussions, and hands-on projects. The flipped classroom not only maximizes face-to-face interactions but also provides students flexibility in engaging with instructional content at their own pace. By leveraging digital tools for asynchronous learning, educators create personalized and adaptive learning environments.

Continuous professional development for educators is crucial for advancing digital classrooms beyond basic integration. In a rapidly evolving technological landscape, educators must update their skills, explore emerging technologies, and refine instructional practices. Targeted professional development programs provide educators with the knowledge and confidence to effectively use advanced digital tools. Collaboration among educators within digital professional learning communities enhances the sharing of best practices, strategies, and innovative approaches. Investing in ongoing professional development empowers educators to unlock the full potential of digital classrooms, ensuring technology remains a powerful tool for transformative teaching and learning.

4.2 E-Learning Platforms: Revolutionizing Accessibility

The rise of technology has brought a significant transformation to education, with E-Learning platforms emerging as pivotal drivers of change. These platforms have gained considerable popularity, reshaped the educational landscape and making learning more accessible worldwide. The traditional classroom setup, with its physical constraints and face-to-face interactions, has been complemented, if not replaced, by the flexible and dynamic nature of E-Learning. This shift has played a crucial role in enhancing accessibility, breaking down barriers, and democratizing education on a global scale.

One of the primary advantages of E-Learning platforms is their ability to eliminate geographical limitations. In traditional education systems, students were often restricted to local institutions, facing challenges in accessing quality education due to distance, limited infrastructure, or financial constraints. E-Learning has revolutionized this aspect by allowing learners to access a diverse array of courses and programs from anywhere in the world. This increased accessibility is particularly transformative for individuals in underserved or remote areas, enabling them to pursue education without needing to relocate.

Furthermore, E-Learning platforms significantly contribute to inclusivity by accommodating diverse learning styles and needs. Traditional classrooms may struggle to cater to individual learning paces and preferences, posing challenges for some students. E-Learning addresses this by offering multimedia content, interactive modules, and adaptive learning technologies that can be tailored to different learning styles. Additionally, accessibility features like closed captioning and transcripts ensure that learners with disabilities can fully participate in the educational process, fostering an inclusive learning environment.

Flexibility is another hallmark of E-Learning platforms that enhances accessibility. In traditional education, rigid schedules and fixed timelines can present barriers for individuals with work obligations, family responsibilities, or other commitments. E-Learning platforms remove these obstacles by allowing learners to set their own pace, enabling them to balance education with other aspects of their lives. This flexibility is especially beneficial for adult learners seeking to advance their skills or pursue higher education while managing professional and personal responsibilities.

Moreover, the cost-effectiveness of E-Learning platforms plays a crucial role in accessibility. Traditional education often entails significant expenses such as tuition fees, accommodation, and commuting costs, which can be prohibitive for many individuals. E-Learning platforms offer a more affordable alternative by eliminating expenses related to physical infrastructure, allowing learners to access quality educational content at a fraction of the cost. This affordability expands educational opportunities to a broader demographic, making learning accessible to those who might otherwise be excluded.

E-Learning also facilitates personalized and adaptive learning experiences tailored to individual strengths, weaknesses, and interests. Through artificial intelligence and data analytics, E-Learning platforms analyze learner performance to customize content and address specific learning needs. This adaptive approach enhances the learning experience and ensures that learners receive the necessary support to succeed.

Personalized learning pathways contribute to improved retention and understanding, making education more accessible and effective for diverse learners.

The global reach of E-Learning platforms promotes cross-cultural collaboration and knowledge exchange. Learners from different parts of the world can engage in discussions, share perspectives, and collaborate on projects, enriching the educational experience with diverse insights. This interconnectedness enhances the quality of education and allows individuals to gain a deeper understanding of different cultures, perspectives, and ways of thinking. The global nature of E-Learning fosters inclusivity, transcending cultural barriers and promoting a more comprehensive understanding of various subjects.

In addition to formal education, E-Learning platforms serve as valuable tools for skill development and vocational training, further enhancing accessibility. Online courses and certifications cover a wide range of skills, from technical and IT skills to soft skills and entrepreneurship. This accessibility to skill-building opportunities is particularly beneficial in a rapidly evolving job market, where continuous learning and adaptability are essential for career advancement.

The incorporation of gamification elements in E-Learning platforms adds engagement and motivation, making learning enjoyable and accessible. Gamified learning modules use badges, points, and leaderboards to incentivize progress and achievement, encouraging learners to stay motivated and engaged. This approach caters to different learning preferences and makes education appealing to a broader audience, including younger learners.

4.3 Virtual Reality and Augmented Reality in Education

Virtual Reality (VR) and Augmented Reality (AR) are ushering in a new era of innovation in education, transforming how students engage with learning materials and interact with their surroundings. These immersive technologies provide educators with powerful tools to create dynamic learning environments that surpass traditional classroom methods. VR, known for its fully immersive digital environments, and AR, which overlays digital content onto the real world, are reshaping education by offering students immersive and interactive experiences that improve understanding, retention, and overall educational outcomes.

One of the main advantages of VR in education is its ability to transport students to places and scenarios that would otherwise be inaccessible. Through VR simulations, students can explore historical events, delve into scientific phenomena, or go on virtual field trips worldwide. This immersion not only boosts engagement but also deepens comprehension of complex concepts. For instance, students studying ancient history can virtually visit ancient civilizations, walking through historical sites and experiencing the culture firsthand. This experiential learning fosters a stronger connection with the subject matter, making education more vivid and memorable.

In contrast, AR enhances the physical world by overlaying digital information onto it, enriching traditional learning materials like textbooks and posters. By scanning a page with a mobile device, students can access additional information, interactive models, or 3D animations related to the content. This interactive approach transforms static materials into engaging learning experiences. For example, a biology textbook page on human anatomy could trigger an AR overlay that allows students to explore 3D models of organs, facilitating a more interactive and comprehensive understanding.

VR and AR also excel in collaborative learning experiences, overcoming the constraints of physical classrooms and fostering global connectivity. With VR, students from different parts of the world can gather virtually to collaborate on projects, engage in discussions, or participate in simulations. This expands the learning environment beyond traditional boundaries and prepares students for a globalized world. In AR, shared augmented experiences allow students to interact with the same augmented content simultaneously, promoting teamwork and communication skills.

The personalized and adaptive capabilities of VR and AR are particularly beneficial for catering to diverse learning styles and abilities. Educators can design immersive experiences that adapt to individual learning paces and preferences, ensuring personalized support. For example, in language learning, VR simulations can provide tailored language immersion experiences adjusted to individual proficiency levels. In AR, personalized content overlays can address specific learning needs, enabling students to focus on areas requiring additional support.

Accessibility in education is another area where VR and AR show promise by providing inclusive learning experiences. These technologies offer alternative modes of interaction and representation for students with different learning abilities or disabilities. In VR, auditory and visual cues can accommodate various learning preferences, while AR's adaptive overlays can include features like text-to-speech functionality. This inclusivity ensures that a broader range of students can engage with educational content in ways that suit their needs, fostering a more equitable learning environment.

Practical skill development is enhanced through VR and AR, offering realistic and safe environments for hands-on training in fields like medicine, aviation, or engineering. VR simulations allow students to practice procedures in virtual settings, refining their skills without real-world consequences. Similarly, AR can guide on-the-job training by overlaying digital instructions onto real-world tasks, boosting proficiency and confidence.

5.4 Gamification: Engaging Learners through Play

Gamification, an approach integrating game elements into non-game contexts, has emerged as a potent strategy for innovative teaching and learning. By harnessing the motivational aspects inherent in games, educators can craft engaging learning experiences that capture students' interest and deepen their grasp of academic content. Elements such as points, badges, leaderboards, and interactive challenges transform classrooms into dynamic spaces where students actively engage in their learning journey.

A primary advantage of gamification in education is its ability to boost motivation and engagement. Games naturally appeal to individuals' desire for challenge, achievement, and recognition, making learning more immersive and enjoyable. Reward systems like points and badges provide instant feedback and a sense of accomplishment, motivating students to invest effort in their studies. This approach is particularly effective in addressing student disengagement and cultivating a positive attitude towards learning.

Additionally, gamification fosters both competition and collaboration among students, adding a social dimension to learning. Leaderboards and team challenges create a friendly competitive environment that encourages students to excel and collaborate. Working together to overcome challenges not only enhances understanding of the subject matter but also builds essential interpersonal skills needed in real-world scenarios.

The element of choice and autonomy inherent in gamification aligns with modern teaching principles. By allowing students to make decisions within educational contexts, gamification accommodates diverse learning styles and preferences. This autonomy empowers learners, giving them control over their educational journey and promoting a personalized approach to teaching.

Moreover, gamification adapts seamlessly to various learning objectives and subjects. Whether teaching scientific concepts, language skills, or historical events, its flexible nature allows for tailored learning experiences. For instance, language learning games may involve translating sentences for points, while science games challenge students with virtual experiments. This versatility enhances the relevance and effectiveness of gamification across different disciplines.

Real-time feedback mechanisms within gamification are invaluable for both educators and students. Immediate feedback enables students to gauge their performance, pinpoint areas for improvement, and adjust their strategies accordingly. Educators benefit from tracking individual progress and can provide timely support to students in need. This data-driven approach creates a responsive learning environment that caters to diverse student needs, ultimately enhancing the overall educational experience.

CHAPTER 5

PROJECT-BASED LEARNING

5.1 Defining Project-Based Learning (PBL)

Project-Based Learning (PBL) represents a transformative educational approach that moves beyond traditional classroom methods by emphasizing the application of knowledge and skills through real-world projects. PBL is not merely a teaching technique but a philosophy aimed at nurturing critical thinking, problem-solving, collaboration, and creativity among students. Unlike conventional learning models focused on memorization, PBL immerses students in hands-on experiences where they grapple with genuine challenges and actively construct knowledge. Its essence lies in bridging the gap between theoretical concepts and practical applications, preparing students for success in today's dynamic world.

At the heart of PBL are projects that serve as pivotal learning experiences. These are not ordinary tasks but intricate endeavors requiring students to deeply explore a topic, integrating knowledge from various disciplines. Whether designing sustainable communities, conducting scientific experiments, or creating multimedia presentations, PBL projects mirror the complexities of real-world problem-solving. Their authenticity not only enhances learning relevance but also instills a sense of purpose and ownership among students.

PBL follows a structured approach guiding students through the entire project lifecycle. It begins with presenting challenging, open-ended questions or problems to spark student curiosity and initiate inquiry. This phase is critical as it stimulates student-driven exploration and investigation. Subsequently, students engage in extensive research, drawing from diverse sources to gather relevant information and insights. This research phase promotes self-directed learning, refining students' abilities to navigate information, evaluate sources critically, and synthesize knowledge effectively.

Collaboration forms a cornerstone of PBL, reflecting the teamwork and interdisciplinary cooperation seen in professional settings. Students collaborate to brainstorm ideas, share perspectives, and pool expertise to tackle complex problems. This collaborative process not only mirrors real-world work environments but also cultivates essential interpersonal skills such as communication, teamwork, and negotiation. Through collaboration, students learn to respect diverse viewpoints, appreciate differing opinions, and leverage each other's strengths-a valuable skill set extending beyond the classroom.

PBL's iterative nature ensures continuous refinement and improvement throughout the project. As students progress, they receive feedback from peers, educators, and sometimes external stakeholders, guiding them in refining their ideas and solutions. This feedback loop fosters a culture of reflection and resilience, where students view challenges as opportunities for growth. The ability to receive constructive feedback and iteratively refine work is a critical skill preparing students for the dynamic nature of the professional world.

In PBL, teachers serve as facilitators and guides rather than mere providers of information. They scaffold the learning experience, offering necessary support, resources, and guidance while empowering students to drive their learning. This shift in the teacher-student dynamic encourages students to take ownership of their education, fostering agency and responsibility. Educators act as mentors, helping students navigate challenges, facilitating discussions, and guiding the overall learning journey.

5.2 Designing Effective PBL Experiences

Designing effective Project-Based Learning (PBL) experiences requires careful planning, thoughtful consideration, and a deep understanding of both the subject matter and the learners. At its core, PBL is about creating immersive, authentic, and meaningful learning journeys that foster critical skills and knowledge acquisition. Successful PBL design involves several key considerations, from setting clear learning objectives and choosing compelling topics to establishing a supportive learning environment and integrating technology seamlessly.

A foundational step in PBL design is identifying clear and measurable learning objectives. These objectives guide the entire project, outlining what students should know, understand, and be able to do by the project's end. Aligning objectives with curriculum standards ensures that the PBL unit fits into the broader educational framework. Well-defined objectives also provide clarity for educators and students alike, outlining the project's purpose and expectations.

Choosing a relevant and engaging topic is crucial for capturing students' interest and creating authenticity in PBL. The topic should resonate with students' interests, connect to real-world issues, and allow exploration across different subjects. A well-chosen topic sparks curiosity, motivates students intrinsically, and frames the learning experience with depth. Whether exploring environmental sustainability, historical events, or community challenges, the topic grounds the project in real-world relevance and purpose.

Central to PBL design is crafting a compelling driving question or problem that serves as the focal point of inquiry. This question should be open-ended, complex, and provoke critical thinking. It prompts students to delve deeply into the subject, conduct research, and apply their knowledge to propose solutions or create artifacts. The driving question initiates inquiry, guiding students through exploration and providing direction to their learning journey.

Creating a supportive and collaborative learning environment is essential for PBL success. Physical and virtual spaces should be conducive to teamwork, discussion, and hands-on exploration. Educators play a key role in fostering a collaborative culture, encouraging students to share ideas, provide peer feedback, and work together towards project goals. A positive and inclusive atmosphere nurtures student ownership and responsibility, enhancing overall project outcomes.

Effective PBL design includes frequent formative assessments to provide ongoing feedback on students' progress. These assessments, such as teacher observations, peer evaluations, or self-reflection activities, gauge individual and group understanding and allow adjustments to project design as needed. This feedback loop promotes continuous improvement, resilience, and reflection among students, reinforcing the dynamic nature of learning.

Technology integration is integral to enhancing PBL effectiveness. Digital tools facilitate research, collaboration, and the creation of multimedia artifacts. Platforms for virtual collaboration enable global connections, broadening project scopes. However, technology should complement learning objectives, enhancing rather than distracting from them. Thoughtful integration empowers students with tools that amplify capabilities and extend project impacts.

Promoting inquiry and research skills is fundamental in PBL. Educators guide students in developing effective research strategies, critically evaluating sources, and synthesizing information. Incorporating primary sources, interviews, and fieldwork enriches the research process, adding authenticity. These skills equip students not only with project-related knowledge but also with lifelong learning skills applicable beyond the classroom.

Reflection is integrated throughout the PBL lifecycle to prompt students to assess progress, identify challenges, and articulate learning experiences. Journaling, group discussions, and reflective essays provide platforms for students to express thoughts, refine understanding, and develop metacognitive skills. Reflection fosters critical thinking about learning processes, enhancing awareness of personal growth and development.

5.3 Assessing and Evaluating PBL Success

Assessing and evaluating the success of Project-Based Learning (PBL) involves a dynamic and comprehensive process that extends beyond traditional grading methods. In the realm of innovative teaching and learning, understanding the impact and effectiveness of PBL experiences requires a thoughtful approach that considers both student outcomes and the overall learning environment. Assessments in PBL aim not only to gauge content mastery but also to evaluate critical skills such as problem-solving, collaboration, and communication – skills essential for thriving in the 21st century.

A fundamental aspect of assessing PBL success is ensuring alignment with defined learning objectives. These objectives form the bedrock of the PBL experience, delineating the knowledge, skills, and competencies students are expected to acquire. Assessment methods should directly reflect these objectives, providing a clear framework for evaluating student achievement. This alignment ensures that assessments arc meaningful, relevant, and directly tied to the overarching goals of the PBL unit.

Authenticity is a guiding principle in PBL assessment, emphasizing the importance of evaluating students in contexts that mirror real-world scenarios. Projects should simulate challenges and tasks encountered in professional environments, allowing students to apply their learning authentically. Assessment criteria should therefore mirror the complexities and expectations of real-world applications, providing a precise measure of students' readiness for future challenges.

Formative assessment plays a pivotal role in PBL, offering ongoing feedback to guide students through their project journeys. These assessments, conducted at various checkpoints, offer insights into individual and group progress, enabling timely adjustments and refinements. Educators play a critical role in providing formative feedback, guiding students in research, problem-solving, and collaboration. Formative assessment not only informs instruction but also empowers students to reflect on their learning processes, fostering continuous improvement.

Peer assessment is another valuable component of PBL evaluation, fostering collaboration, communication, and interpersonal skills development. Through peer evaluations, students gain insights into their strengths and areas for improvement, while also providing constructive feedback to peers. This reciprocal process enhances teamwork, cultivates a sense of shared responsibility, and prepares students for collaborative dynamics in professional settings. Clear criteria and guidelines for peer assessment ensure fairness and objectivity.

In addition to individual assessments, evaluating group dynamics and collaboration is essential in PBL. Group projects are integral to the PBL approach, and assessing collaborative efforts provides a holistic view of students' capabilities. Rubrics for group assessment should encompass factors like communication, teamwork, task allocation, and overall project quality. Recognizing and rewarding effective collaboration reinforces the significance of interpersonal skills and teamwork in the PBL environment.

A comprehensive evaluation of PBL success involves considering not just the final product but also the entire process. Reflective assessments prompt students to articulate their learning experiences, challenges faced, and insights gained throughout the project. This metacognitive approach enhances students' self-awareness and deepens their understanding of learning processes. Reflection can take various forms, such as written reflections, presentations, or group discussions, accommodating diverse learning styles.

Innovative teaching prioritizes the development of critical thinking skills, and PBL assessments should reflect this focus. Evaluation methods should move beyond mere memorization and assess students' abilities to analyze information critically and apply knowledge in novel contexts. Open-ended questions, problem-solving scenarios, and synthesizing information into meaningful solutions serve as effective assessment tools aligned with the cognitive demands of PBL.

When assessing PBL success, it's crucial to value the learning journey rather than solely focusing on the end result. Mastery-oriented assessment approaches emphasize growth, progress, and skill development over time. Recognizing the iterative nature of PBL – where students receive feedback, iterate on their work, and refine solutions – fosters a growth mindset, promoting resilience and continuous improvement.

External stakeholder feedback adds authenticity to PBL assessments. Involving professionals, community members, or subject matter experts in evaluating student projects enhances the relevance of assessments and exposes students to diverse perspectives. External feedback validates project authenticity, reinforces the link between academic learning and real-world applications, and provides valuable insights from industry professionals.

CHAPTER 6

FLIPPING THE CLASSROOM

6.1 Understanding the Flipped Classroom Model

The flipped classroom model represents a revolutionary approach to education that challenges traditional teaching structures. Unlike the conventional method where students receive lectures in class and complete homework independently, the flipped model flips this sequence. Here, instructional content like pre-recorded videos or readings is delivered outside of class, enabling students to engage with the material at their own pace before attending class. Classroom time is then utilized for interactive, Student-centred learning activities, discussions, and collaborative projects facilitated by the teacher. This inversion aims to optimize face-to-face sessions for deeper comprehension, application, and exploration of concepts, creating a more dynamic and engaging learning environment.

Central to the flipped classroom model is the idea that direct instruction can effectively occur through various media outside of class, offering students a personalized and flexible learning experience. Learners have the freedom to access instructional materials at times and speeds that suit their individual learning styles and preferences. Whether watching video lectures, reading articles, or exploring interactive online modules, students can review and revisit content until they grasp the concepts, promoting a self-directed approach to learning. This flexibility accommodates diverse learning needs and ensures all students can absorb foundational knowledge at their own pace.

In traditional classrooms, time is often dominated by lectures, limiting opportunities for active participation and collaboration. In contrast, the flipped model transforms the classroom into an active space for Student-centred learning activities. Class time becomes a platform for in-depth discussions, problem-solving, hands-on experiments, and collaborative projects. This shift from passive reception to active engagement not only enhances understanding but also nurtures critical thinking, communication, and teamwork skills – crucial competencies for success in today's world.

Moreover, the flipped classroom empowers educators to adopt a flexible teaching style. Instead of delivering uniform lectures to passive listeners, teachers can tailor in-class activities to address the specific needs and challenges of individual students. This personalized approach enables educators to offer targeted support, clarify doubts, and facilitate deeper discussions based on each student's unique learning journey. As a result, teachers assume the role of facilitators, guiding students through complex tasks and cultivating a more interactive and stimulating educational experience.

Furthermore, the flipped classroom model enhances opportunities for differentiation and scaffolding. With instructional content available outside class time, teachers can design activities that cater to diverse skill levels and learning needs during face-to-face sessions. Advanced students can tackle more challenging tasks, while those requiring extra support receive focused assistance and reinforcement. This approach promotes inclusivity, ensuring all students access appropriate resources and opportunities for growth, regardless of their starting point.

Technology integration is pivotal to the success of the flipped classroom model. Digital platforms, learning management systems, and multimedia tools facilitate the creation and dissemination of instructional materials. Educators can utilize a range of resources such as video lectures, podcasts, e-books, and interactive simulations to deliver content in engaging formats. Additionally, technology enables seamless communication and collaboration among students and instructors, fostering a sense of community and connectivity in the learning process.

6.2 Creating Engaging Pre-Class Materials

Designing engaging pre-class materials is crucial in modern educational strategies, especially within the flipped classroom model. The success of this approach relies heavily on the quality and appeal of the materials students interact with before attending class. These resources lay the groundwork for self-guided learning, equipping students with essential content to build a solid understanding of the subject matter. Creating compelling pre-class materials involves careful consideration of several elements, including how content is delivered, the integration of multimedia, alignment with learning goals, and opportunities for interaction and reflection.

Firstly, the method chosen to deliver content significantly impacts engagement. Educators must select approaches that resonate with diverse learning styles. Video lectures offer a dynamic, visual connection between instructor and learner, while written texts cater to those preferring a reflective approach. Offering a variety of methods ensures accessibility and engagement for all students.

Integrating multimedia enhances engagement further by reinforcing concepts through multiple sensory channels. For instance, animations can clarify complex processes, complementing textual explanations and aiding comprehension. Well-chosen multimedia not only captures attention but also deepens understanding.

Aligning materials with learning objectives is crucial for relevance. Content should directly support lesson goals, ensuring students grasp essential concepts. This alignment clarifies the purpose of pre-class materials within the curriculum, guiding students towards specific learning outcomes.

Interactive elements transform passive consumption into active learning experiences. Embedded quizzes, discussion prompts, and links to additional resources keep students engaged and encourage self-assessment. These features promote deeper understanding and preparation for class discussions.

Reflection prompts within materials encourage students to connect content with prior knowledge or real-world applications. This process enhances metacognitive skills and prepares students for meaningful participation in classroom activities.

Real-world relevance adds authenticity by demonstrating practical implications of learning. For instance, historical lessons can include primary sources to illustrate impact on current issues, making content more engaging and meaningful beyond the classroom.

Clear organization and structure facilitate ease of use. Headings, subheadings, and overviews help students navigate materials effectively, reducing cognitive load and enhancing focus on content.

Lastly, feedback mechanisms ensure continuous improvement. Gathering student input on clarity and effectiveness allows educators to refine materials iteratively. Monitoring engagement metrics provides insights for timely adjustments, ensuring ongoing effectiveness.

6.3 Maximizing In-Class Time for Application and Discussion

Emphasizing active engagement and collaborative learning in classrooms is a cornerstone of modern educational methods, particularly in the context of the flipped classroom approach. This innovative model challenges traditional teaching practices by encouraging students to prepare with materials beforehand, thereby freeing up valuable in-class time for deeper and more interactive learning activities.

The concept behind the flipped classroom is simple yet transformative: rather than spending class time primarily on delivering content, educators provide instructional materials for students to study independently before coming to class. This pre-class preparation allows students to absorb foundational knowledge at their own pace, ensuring that when they gather in person, they are ready to engage in higher-order thinking, problem-solving, and hands-on applications.

By utilizing this approach, educators can shift their focus from transmitting information to facilitating dynamic learning experiences. In-class sessions become opportunities for students to actively apply their understanding of concepts through activities such as experiments, group projects, case studies, and discussions. For example, in a science class, students might conduct experiments that apply theoretical knowledge to real-world scenarios, fostering a deeper appreciation of how concepts manifest in practical settings.

Collaborative activities are a pivotal component of maximizing the benefits of in-class time. By engaging in group projects, discussions, and peer interactions, students not only share diverse perspectives but also develop essential teamwork and communication skills. This collaborative environment mirrors professional settings, preparing students for future careers where teamwork and communication are paramount.

Moreover, in-depth discussions serve as a hallmark of effective classroom engagement. Encouraging students to articulate their thoughts, question assumptions, and explore alternative viewpoints fosters critical thinking and intellectual growth. Socratic seminars, debates, and interactive discussions are powerful tools for cultivating these skills, deepening students' understanding of content while enhancing their ability to communicate effectively.

In addition to active learning strategies, formative assessments play a crucial role in maximizing in-class time. These assessments provide immediate feedback to both educators and students, highlighting areas where further clarification or support may be needed. By addressing misunderstandings in real-time, educators can tailor their instructional approach to meet the specific needs of their students, ensuring that every moment spent in class is productive and enriching.

Technology integration further enhances the classroom experience by facilitating communication, collaboration, and access to resources. Digital tools and learning management systems enable educators to share materials, facilitate discussions, and even conduct virtual simulations that immerse students in interactive learning experiences. For instance, virtual reality can transport history students to different eras, providing a vivid and engaging way to explore historical contexts.

Creating flexible learning spaces is another key consideration in optimizing in-class time. By designing classrooms with adaptable seating arrangements and interactive technologies, educators can accommodate diverse instructional activities and learning preferences. This flexibility aligns with the dynamic nature of modern teaching practices, ensuring that the physical environment supports varied modes of learning and interaction.

6.4 Challenges and Solutions

Transitioning to a flipped classroom presents educators with both challenges and opportunities that require careful consideration for successful implementation. This innovative approach reverses traditional teaching methods by delivering instructional content outside of class, thereby utilizing in-person sessions for interactive application and discussion. This shift holds promise for enhancing student engagement and deepening comprehension but necessitates overcoming several obstacles.

One significant challenge is ensuring that students are prepared and accountable for reviewing materials before class. Asynchronous learning demands self-discipline and motivation from students, who may struggle with the responsibility of independent study. To address this, educators can establish clear expectations, stress the importance of pre-class preparation, and implement measures like quizzes to encourage readiness.

Access to technology poses another hurdle, as not all students may have equal access to devices or reliable internet. This digital disparity can undermine the effectiveness of the flipped model. To mitigate this issue, educators should consider alternative content delivery methods, provide offline resources, and collaborate with institutions to bridge technology gaps.

Creating high-quality pre-class materials also requires significant time and effort from educators, which can be daunting. Collaborating with peers, utilizing existing resources, and incorporating student-generated content can lighten this load while promoting active student involvement.

Moreover, shifting from a lecturer-centered to a facilitator-centered approach challenges both educators and students. Educators may struggle to relinquish control over content delivery, while students may initially resist taking on a more active role in their learning. Professional development and clear communication are essential to supporting educators through this transition and helping students embrace their new roles.

Maximizing in-class time for meaningful activities and discussions involves careful planning and management. Educators must accommodate diverse learning styles and preferences while balancing group work and individualized support. Strategies such as differentiated instruction and technology integration can facilitate this process.

Assessment in a flipped classroom also presents unique considerations.

Traditional exams may not align with active learning approaches, necessitating the development of assessments that authentically evaluate critical thinking and application of knowledge. Providing timely feedback becomes crucial in guiding student progress.

CHAPTER 7

EXPERIENTIAL LEARNING

7.1 Learning by Doing: A Holistic Approach

This educational philosophy transforms traditional teaching methods into dynamic and engaging experiences by emphasizing active participation, hands-on learning, and real-world applications to foster deep understanding of concepts. Students are encouraged to learn through direct experience, exploring, experimenting, and discovering knowledge independently.

A key principle is integrating theory with practical application. Instead of relying solely on textbooks and lectures, students engage in activities promoting critical thinking and problem-solving. For example, in a science class, students might grow gardens to observe photosynthesis firsthand, linking theoretical knowledge with tangible experiences, enhancing retention and enjoyment of learning.

Moreover, this approach goes beyond subject-specific content to emphasize life skills such as communication, teamwork, and adaptability. Group projects, simulations, and collaborative activities are essential, preparing students for real-world challenges. This "Learning by Doing" approach fosters academic growth and personal and social development.

Recognizing diverse learning styles, educators offer varied experiences like visual aids, hands-on activities, and interactive discussions to cater to different ways students learn. This inclusivity ensures every student has the chance to thrive.

Innovative teaching tools like virtual simulations, augmented reality, and online platforms are crucial for implementing this pedagogy. They create immersive learning experiences that simulate real-world scenarios, such as exploring ancient civilizations in history class, preparing students for future careers in a digital age.

Continuous assessment and feedback are integral, moving beyond traditional exams to evaluate participation, problem-solving, and critical thinking skills. This ongoing evaluation provides a comprehensive understanding of students' strengths and areas needing improvement, guiding targeted support.

A notable benefit of "Learning by Doing" is its ability to ignite a genuine passion for learning. When students are actively engaged and see the relevance of their studies, they develop curiosity that extends beyond the classroom, motivating lifelong learning.

Furthermore, this approach meets modern workforce demands by preparing students with both academic knowledge and practical skills. It equips them to apply knowledge effectively in real-world settings, aligning with expectations in today's professional landscape where practical application is highly valued.

7.2 Integrating Internships and Fieldwork

Integrating internships and fieldwork into educational programs represents a forward-thinking approach to learning that extends beyond traditional classrooms. This approach recognizes the importance of real-world experiences in shaping students' understanding and skills. By offering internships and fieldwork, educators help students bridge the gap between theory and practice, allowing them to immerse themselves in professional settings.

One of the main advantages of internships and fieldwork is the hands-on experience they provide. Instead of relying solely on textbooks, students gain practical insights by participating in real-world activities.

For instance, a student studying environmental science might conduct fieldwork to collect and analyze soil samples, acquiring skills that textbooks alone cannot teach.

Additionally, internships and fieldwork bring academic learning to life by providing context and relevance. When students can observe and apply classroom concepts in actual work environments, their understanding deepens. This connection between theory and practice improves comprehension and retention, as students witness firsthand how their academic knowledge applies to real-world situations.

Moreover, these experiences help students develop essential soft skills such as communication, teamwork, problem-solving, and adaptability. Engaging in diverse work environments challenges students to collaborate effectively and navigate professional complexities. These skills are crucial not only for career success but also for personal growth.

Furthermore, internships and fieldwork facilitate networking opportunities for students. By interacting with professionals in their field, students build connections that can lead to future job opportunities and mentorship. These experiences provide insights into industry practices that are invaluable for students' career development.

Integrating internships and fieldwork into educational frameworks also meets the evolving demands of the job market. Employers increasingly value candidates with practical experience, and these opportunities ensure that students graduate with both academic knowledge and applicable skills. Exposure to real-world challenges prepares students to enter the workforce confidently and competitively.

Moreover, internships and fieldwork contribute to a well-rounded education by fostering lifelong learning and adaptability. Students exposed to different work environments develop resilience and a mindset of continuous improvement, which are essential in a rapidly changing world.

Educators play a crucial role in facilitating internships and fieldwork experiences by collaborating with industry partners and guiding students through reflective processes. By helping students connect their experiences to academic theories, educators enhance the transformative impact of internships and fieldwork on student learning.

7.3 The Role of Reflection in Experiential Learning

Reflection plays a crucial role in experiential learning, enriching the educational experience by deepening understanding and promoting personal growth. Experiential learning emphasizes hands-on activities and active participation, with reflection serving as a vital link that connects these experiences to deeper insights.

The primary function of reflection is to enhance the learning process. When students engage in real-world activities like internships or hands-on projects, they encounter situations that challenge their existing knowledge. Reflection allows students to revisit these experiences mentally, analyzing the complexities involved and identifying new insights. By critically examining their experiences, students gain a more profound understanding of the subject matter.

Additionally, reflection promotes metacognition-the awareness of one's own thinking processes. By encouraging students to reflect on their experiences, educators help them understand their learning styles, strengths, and areas needing improvement. This self-awareness empowers students to take charge of their learning journey, preparing them to succeed in diverse academic and professional settings.

Reflection also bridges the gap between academic theory and practical application. In traditional learning environments, theory and practice are often disconnected. Through reflection, students can connect their experiences to theoretical concepts, demonstrating the relevance and applicability of their academic learning in real-world contexts.

Moreover, reflection fosters critical thinking skills. As students reflect on their experiences, they analyze, evaluate, and synthesize information, developing a deeper understanding of complex issues. This critical reflection nurtures the ability to think critically and make informed decisions, which are essential skills for academic and professional success.

Furthermore, reflection contributes to emotional and personal growth. Experiential learning involves encountering challenges and successes that evoke various emotions. Reflective practices enable students to explore these emotional responses, gaining insights into their values, beliefs, and motivations. This emotional intelligence enhances the holistic development of learners, promoting resilience and personal well-being.

In practice, reflection is an active and ongoing process in experiential learning. Educators employ various methods such as journaling, group discussions, and multimedia presentations to facilitate reflection. These diverse approaches cater to different learning styles, ensuring that all students can engage meaningfully in reflective practices.

Additionally, integrating reflection into the assessment process enhances the authenticity of evaluating student learning. Instead of relying solely on traditional exams, educators can assess students based on their ability to critically reflect on their experiences. This holistic approach not only measures knowledge acquisition but also evaluates the application of knowledge and the development of essential skills like critical thinking and communication.

CHAPTER 8

ASSESSING INNOVATIVE PEDAGOGY

8.1 Rethinking Assessment in Modern Education

Rethinking assessment in modern education is a crucial aspect of innovative teaching and learning pedagogy. Traditionally, assessments have been synonymous with exams and standardized tests, often measuring a student's ability to memorize information rather than their true understanding and application of knowledge. However, the evolving landscape of education recognizes the limitations of this approach and calls for a paradigm shift towards more dynamic and authentic assessment methods. Innovative teaching and learning pedagogy advocate for assessments that go beyond rote memorization and focus on evaluating critical thinking, problem-solving, and practical skills. This shift acknowledges the importance of preparing students for the complexities of the real world, where the ability to apply knowledge in diverse situations is paramount. For instance, project-based assessments, where students work on real-world problems or create tangible solutions, provide a more holistic understanding of their capabilities.

Furthermore, rethinking assessment involves embracing formative assessment strategies that provide continuous feedback throughout the learning process. This ongoing evaluation allows educators to identify students' strengths and areas for improvement in real-time, facilitating a more personalized and targeted approach to instruction. Formative assessments can take various forms, including quizzes, discussions, and peer reviews, creating a comprehensive picture of a student's progress beyond the constraints of a final exam.

The integration of technology plays a pivotal role in reimagining assessment methods. Online platforms, simulations, and digital portfolios offer interactive and dynamic ways to evaluate students' understanding and skills. Technology-driven assessments can simulate real-world scenarios, allowing students to showcase their abilities in a virtual environment. Moreover, these tools enable educators to gather and analyze data efficiently, fostering data-informed decision-making to enhance the learning experience.

Authentic assessments, such as case studies and real-world projects, provide students with opportunities to demonstrate their abilities in practical contexts. These assessments mirror the challenges professionals face in their respective fields, bridging the gap between academic learning and real-world application. Authentic assessments not only measure subject knowledge but also develop students' problem-solving, critical thinking, and communication skills, preparing them for success in their future careers. Additionally, student involvement in the assessment process is a key aspect of rethinking evaluation methods. Encouraging self-assessment and reflection empowers students to take ownership of their learning journey. Peer assessment, where students evaluate their classmates' work, promotes collaboration and a deeper understanding of the subject matter. These collaborative evaluation approaches align with the principles of innovative pedagogy, fostering a sense of responsibility and engagement among students.

The concept of competency-based assessment is gaining traction in modern education. Instead of relying solely on grades, competency-based assessment focuses on students' mastery of specific skills and knowledge. This approach allows for a more granular understanding of a student's strengths and areas for improvement, providing a comprehensive view of their abilities. Competency-based assessment also emphasizes the development of lifelong learning skills, as students continually strive to enhance their proficiency in specific competencies.

Furthermore, rethinking assessment involves recognizing and valuing diverse forms of intelligence and skills. Traditional assessments often prioritize linguistic and mathematical intelligence, neglecting other valuable abilities such as creativity, emotional intelligence, and practical skills. Innovative pedagogy encourages a more inclusive approach to assessment that acknowledges and evaluates a wide range of talents, fostering a more equitable and diverse educational landscape.

8.2 Formative and Summative Assessment in Innovative Pedagogy

Innovative teaching and learning pedagogy emphasizes the dual role of formative and summative assessments as integral components of the educational landscape. Formative assessment, characterized by ongoing and interactive evaluation, serves as a dynamic tool for educators to gauge student progress during the learning process. This approach allows for timely feedback, enabling instructors to identify strengths and areas for improvement in real-time. Formative assessments take various forms, such as quizzes, discussions, projects, and peer evaluations, fostering a more holistic understanding of students' comprehension and skills. By embracing formative assessments, educators create a responsive and Student-centred environment, tailoring instruction to individual needs and promoting a deeper engagement with the material.

Summative assessment, on the other hand, encapsulates a comprehensive evaluation of students' overall learning outcomes at the end of an instructional period. Unlike formative assessments, summative assessments are typically more formal and often include final exams, standardized tests, or culminating projects. While formative assessments provide ongoing insights, summative assessments offer a holistic view of a student's mastery of a subject or course. This approach aids in making informed decisions about a student's progression, grading, and readiness for further academic or professional pursuits. Summative assessments serve as benchmarks, measuring the effectiveness of the entire learning process and providing valuable insights for curriculum refinement.

The synergy between formative and summative assessments is a hallmark of innovative pedagogy. Formative assessments inform instructional strategies, allowing educators to adapt and refine their teaching methods based on real-time feedback. They enable a continuous feedback loop, fostering a dynamic and responsive learning environment. In contrast, summative assessments provide a comprehensive snapshot of a student's overall achievement and serve as a valuable tool for accountability and program evaluation.

The incorporation of technology enhances the effectiveness of formative and summative assessments in innovative pedagogy. Digital platforms and tools offer interactive ways to conduct formative assessments, such as online quizzes, polls, and collaborative platforms. These tools not only streamline the assessment process but also provide immediate feedback, enabling students to address gaps in their understanding promptly. Additionally, technology facilitates the analysis of data collected from formative assessments, offering valuable insights for instructional improvement and individualized support.

Innovative pedagogy encourages a shift in the mindset surrounding assessments, emphasizing the educational value of both formative and summative evaluations. Formative assessments are not only checkpoints for progress but opportunities for students to actively engage with the learning process. Educators can leverage formative assessments to encourage critical thinking, collaboration, and self-reflection. Moreover, by involving students in the assessment process through self-assessment and peer evaluation, a sense of responsibility and ownership over learning outcomes is fostered.

Summative assessments, while providing a comprehensive overview of a student's proficiency, are viewed as more than mere end-of-course evaluations. Innovative pedagogy recognizes the potential for summative assessments to be transformative learning experiences. Culminating projects, portfolio assessments, and presentations can serve as opportunities for students to showcase their acquired skills, apply knowledge in real-world contexts, and demonstrate a deep understanding of the subject matter. This approach not only enhances the authenticity of assessments but also prepares students for the demands of future academic and professional endeavors.

An integral aspect of formative assessments within innovative pedagogy is the emphasis on continuous improvement. Educators utilize the insights gained from formative assessments to adjust instructional methods, modify learning activities, and address the diverse needs of students. The focus is not solely on grading but on creating a supportive and adaptive learning environment. This iterative process aligns with the principles of lifelong learning, encouraging students to view assessments as opportunities for growth rather than mere indicators of performance.

Summative assessments, while providing a culminating evaluation, also contribute to the ongoing evolution of education. Through careful analysis of summative assessment data, educators can identify trends, assess the effectiveness of instructional approaches, and make informed decisions about curriculum design and delivery. This cyclical process of assessment and refinement ensures that education remains responsive to the evolving needs of students, society, and the workforce.

CHAPTER 9

CASE STUDIES IN INNOVATION

9.1 Success Stories in Implementing Innovative Pedagogy

In the realm of education, success stories in implementing innovative pedagogy serve as beacons of inspiration, illustrating the transformative power of forward-thinking approaches. One compelling example comes from a school district that wholeheartedly embraced project-based learning (PBL). Departing from traditional lecture-style teaching, educators here designed curricula that immersed students in real-world projects, fostering critical thinking, collaboration, and problem-solving skills. The impact was profound, with students not only showcasing a deeper understanding of academic content but also exhibiting heightened motivation and enthusiasm for learning. Test scores improved, but more importantly, this initiative produced graduates who were not merely recipients of information but active, engaged learners prepared for the challenges beyond the classroom.

Similarly, a university's success story unfolded through the adoption of flipped classroom techniques. Instructors utilized digital resources to deliver content online before class, utilizing in-person sessions for interactive discussions, collaborative activities, and hands-on applications of knowledge. This innovative approach not only enhanced student engagement but also allowed for more personalized support, as instructors addressed individual needs during face-to-face interactions. The result was a notable improvement in student retention rates and an overall positive impact on academic performance. This success story highlights how a shift in the traditional teaching model can lead to profound improvements in the learning experience.

In the technology integration domain, a school district implemented a one-to-one device program, providing each student with a personal laptop or tablet. Beyond basic research, these devices became tools for interactive simulations, virtual reality experiences, and online collaboration, transforming the learning process. Students not only became proficient in using technology but also learned to leverage it for creativity and critical thinking, preparing them for the digital demands of the 21st century. This success story emphasizes that technology, when integrated strategically, can be a catalyst for enriching the educational experience.

Inclusive education takes center stage in another success story, where a school implemented a Universal Design for Learning (UDL) framework. Recognizing the diverse needs of students, educators employed multiple means of representation, engagement, and expression in their teaching. The UDL approach catered to various learning styles and addressed the needs of students with varying abilities. The school witnessed a significant reduction in achievement gaps, and students with disabilities reported feeling more included and supported in their academic journey. This success story underscores the importance of inclusivity in educational practices, demonstrating that when the learning environment is tailored to diverse needs, every student can thrive.

A collaborative effort between educators, policymakers, and industry stakeholders yielded impressive results in preparing students for the workforce. A school district partnered with local businesses to create internship programs, allowing students to gain real-world experience and develop practical skills. Policymakers played a crucial role in facilitating such collaborations by providing the necessary framework and support. As a result, students not only graduated with academic knowledge but also with a tangible skill set that made them highly marketable in the job market. This success story showcases the power of collaboration in bridging the gap between classroom learning and real-world application, illustrating that partnerships with industry can be a key component of an effective educational strategy.

Flexibility and adaptability in education emerge as themes in another success story where a high school embraced a flexible scheduling system. Students were given the opportunity to pursue their interests through a combination of traditional classes, online courses, and independent projects. This flexibility not only accommodated diverse learning styles but also empowered students to take ownership of their education. Graduation rates increased, and students reported higher levels of satisfaction with their learning experiences. This success story challenges traditional notions of rigid academic structures and demonstrates the positive outcomes that can arise from embracing a more flexible and Student-centred approach.

9.2 Collaboration Among Educators, Policymakers, and Industry

In the realm of innovative teaching and learning pedagogy, a fundamental transformation is underway as educators, policymakers, and industry stakeholders recognize the imperative of collaboration. Traditionally, these entities have operated in silos, but the current educational landscape demands a more interconnected and synergistic approach. The convergence of expertise from educators, policymakers shaping educational directives, and industry professionals driving the demands of the workforce is seen as pivotal in crafting pedagogical strategies that not only meet academic standards but also prepare students for the dynamic challenges of the real world.

Educators are increasingly engaging in collaborative efforts with policymakers to bridge the gap between theory and practice.

Policymakers, understanding the nuanced needs of the education sector, are seeking input from educators who are at the forefront of the classroom. This collaboration allows for the development of policies that are not only informed by educational research but are also grounded in the practical experiences of those responsible for implementing them. The result is a more responsive and adaptable educational framework that aligns with the evolving needs of students and society.

Moreover, the integration of industry perspectives into the educational discourse is becoming a cornerstone of innovative teaching and learning pedagogy. Industry professionals bring valuable insights into the skills and competencies that are in high demand in the job market. Collaborative initiatives involving educators, policymakers, and industry stakeholders enable the identification of essential skills beyond academic knowledge-skills such as critical thinking, problem-solving, communication, and adaptability. By incorporating industry perspectives, educators can tailor their pedagogical approaches to ensure that students are not only academically proficient but also equipped with the practical skills that will make them valuable contributors to the workforce.

Partnerships between educators and industry also extend beyond curriculum design. Collaborative initiatives, such as internships, mentorship programs, and industry-sponsored projects, provide students with real-world exposure and experiences. These hands-on opportunities allow students to apply theoretical knowledge in practical settings, fostering a deeper understanding of the subject matter and enhancing their readiness for the professional world. Simultaneously, industry professionals gain insight into the potential of the emerging workforce, influencing their own practices and contributing to a cyclical process of improvement and collaboration.

Policy decisions play a crucial role in shaping the educational landscape, and collaboration between educators and policymakers is essential for creating effective, Student-centred policies. This collaborative effort goes beyond simply implementing directives; it involves a continuous feedback loop where educators contribute their insights to refine and improve policies. Policymakers, in turn, gain a clearer understanding of the challenges faced in the classroom, enabling them to make informed decisions that positively impact teaching and learning outcomes.

Furthermore, the dynamic nature of the modern workforce requires a more agile and responsive education system. Collaborative efforts among educators, policymakers, and industry professionals facilitate the identification of emerging trends and changing skill requirements. This collective intelligence allows for the timely adaptation of curricula and teaching methodologies to align with the evolving needs of the job market. The result is an educational system that produces graduates who are not only academically proficient but also well-prepared to navigate the complexities of a rapidly changing global economy.

In the context of innovative teaching and learning pedagogy, collaborative initiatives also extend to the realm of research and development. Educators working hand-in-hand with researchers, policymakers, and industry experts can conduct studies that provide valuable insights into effective teaching methodologies, the impact of technology on learning outcomes, and the most relevant skills for future success. This collaborative research contributes to evidence-based practices, informing educational policies and shaping the direction of innovative pedagogical approaches.

CONCLUSION

In conclusion, the exploration of Innovative Teaching and Learning Pedagogy unveils a paradigm shift in education, emphasizing dynamic approaches that go beyond traditional boundaries. The pillars of this innovation, as delineated in the various chapters, encapsulate a holistic transformation in how educators conceive and deliver knowledge. From prioritizing Student-centred Learning and integrating technology strategically to fostering inclusivity in diverse learning environments, the pedagogical landscape is evolving to meet the demands of the 21st century. Teachers, once seen as imparting information, are now acknowledged as architects of innovation, navigating changing roles, embracing growth mindsets, and fostering collaborative communities. Technology emerges not only as a catalyst for change but as a fundamental tool in creating immersive and engaging learning experiences. Specific pedagogical models, including Project-Based Learning, Flipped Classrooms, and Experiential Learning, highlight the importance of hands-on, application-oriented education. The imperative of inclusive education strategies and the rethinking of assessment methods underscore a commitment to ensuring every learner's success. Real-world case studies offer tangible evidence of the transformative impact of innovative practices, celebrating successes, learning from failures, and measuring tangible impacts on student achievement. The journey culminates in the exploration of scaling innovations, recognizing the need for widespread dissemination, policy implications, and collaborative efforts among educators, policymakers, and industry stakeholders. Innovative teaching and learning pedagogy thus represents a holistic and forward-thinking approach, reshaping education to nurture adaptable, critical-thinking individuals ready to thrive in an ever-evolving world. As we continue to navigate the complexities of education, these insights serve as a compass, guiding educators, policymakers, and stakeholders towards an inclusive, dynamic, and effective educational future.

REFERENCES

1. Dewey, J. (1938). "Experience and Education." New York: Macmillan.
2. Kolb, D. A. (1984). "Experiential Learning: Experience as the Source of Learning and Development." Englewood Cliffs, NJ: Prentice-Hall.
3. Vygotsky, L. S. (1978). "Mind in Society: The Development of Higher Psychological Processes." Cambridge, MA: Harvard University Press.
4. Freire, P. (1970). "Pedagogy of the Oppressed." New York: Continuum.
5. Bloom, B. S. (1956). "Taxonomy of Educational Objectives, Handbook I: The Cognitive Domain." New York: David McKay Co Inc.
6. Gardner, H. (1983). "Frames of Mind: The Theory of Multiple Intelligences." New York: Basic Books.
7. Bransford, J. D., Brown, A. L., & Cocking, R. R. (Eds.). (2000). "How People Learn: Brain, Mind, Experience, and School." Washington, DC: National Academy Press.
8. Piaget, J. (1952). "The Origins of Intelligence in Children." New York: International Universities Press.
9. Ausubel, D. P. (1968). "Educational Psychology: A Cognitive View." New York: Holt, Rinehart and Winston.
10. Bandura, A. (1977). "Social Learning Theory." Englewood Cliffs, NJ: Prentice Hall.
11. Merrill, M. D. (2002). "First Principles of Instruction." Educational Technology Research and Development, 50(3), 43-59.
12. Siemens, G. (2005). "Connectivism: A Learning Theory for the

Digital Age." International Journal of Instructional Technology and Distance Learning, 2(1), 3-10.

13. Laurillard, D. (2002). "Rethinking University Teaching: A Conversational Framework for the Effective Use of Learning Technologies." London: Routledge.
14. Knowles, M. S., Holton, E. F., & Swanson, R. A. (2015). "The Adult Learner: The Definitive Classic in Adult Education and Human Resource Development." New York: Routledge.
15. Schunk, D. H. (2012). "Learning Theories: An Educational Perspective." Boston: Pearson.
16. Garrison, D. R., & Vaughan, N. D. (2008). "Blended Learning in Higher Education: Framework, Principles, and Guidelines." San Francisco: Jossey-Bass.
17. Johnson, D. W., Johnson, R. T., & Smith, K. A. (1991). "Cooperative Learning: Increasing College Faculty Instructional Productivity." ASHE-ERIC Higher Education Report No. 4. Washington, DC: George Washington University.
18. Bonwell, C. C., & Eison, J. A. (1991). "Active Learning: Creating Excitement in the Classroom." ASHE-ERIC Higher Education Report No. 1. Washington, DC: George Washington University.
19. Chickering, A. W., & Gamson, Z. F. (1987). "Seven Principles for Good Practice in Undergraduate Education." AAHE Bulletin, 39(7), 3-7.
20. Brookfield, S. D. (2015). "The Skillful Teacher: On Technique, Trust, and Responsiveness in the Classroom." San Francisco: Jossey-Bass.
21. Biggs, J., & Tang, C. (2011). "Teaching for Quality Learning at University: What the Student Does." Maidenhead: Open University Press.

22. Entwistle, N. (2009). "Teaching for Understanding at University: Deep Approaches and Distinctive Ways of Thinking." London: Palgrave Macmillan.
23. Ramsden, P. (2003). "Learning to Teach in Higher Education." London: Routledge.
24. Hattie, J. (2009). "Visible Learning: A Synthesis of Over 800 Meta-Analyses Relating to Achievement." London: Routledge.
25. Tinto, V. (1993). "Leaving College: Rethinking the Causes and Cures of Student Attrition." Chicago: University of Chicago Press.
26. Mezirow, J. (1991). "Transformative Dimensions of Adult Learning." San Francisco: Jossey-Bass.
27. Ericsson, K. A., Krampe, R. T., & Tesch-Römer, C. (1993). "The Role of Deliberate Practice in the Acquisition of Expert Performance." Psychological Review, 100(3), 363-406.
28. Brown, P. C., Roediger III, H. L., & McDaniel, M. A. (2014). "Make It Stick: The Science of Successful Learning." Cambridge, MA: Harvard University Press.
29. Mazur, E. (1997). "Peer Instruction: A User's Manual." Upper Saddle River, NJ: Prentice Hall.
30. Bates, T. (2015). "Teaching in a Digital Age: Guidelines for Designing Teaching and Learning." Vancouver, BC: Tony Bates Associates Ltd.
31. Rao, V. (2011). "Learning and Teaching: The International Perspective on Redefining the Indian Education System." New Delhi: Pearson Education India.
32. Kumar, S. (2013). "Innovative Pedagogies for Teacher Education." New Delhi: APH Publishing Corporation.
33. Roy, R. (2018). "Integrating ICT in Teaching-Learning: Experiences from Indian Classrooms." New Delhi: Sage

Publications India.

34. Aggarwal, J. C. (2009). "Essentials of Educational Technology: Teaching Learning Innovations in Education." New Delhi: Vikas Publishing House Pvt Ltd.
35. Sharma, R. C. (2006). "Modern Science Teaching." New Delhi: Dhanpat Rai Publications.

www.ingramcontent.com/pod-product-compliance
Lightning Source LLC
LaVergne TN
LVHW031427170726
843492LV00009B/2891

* 9 7 8 8 1 9 7 7 9 2 7 3 1 *